HOW BIRDS LIVE

Tony Bremner

Quetzal

Harpy
Eagle

Keel-billed
Toucan

Consultant Editor
Peter Olney, B.Sc., Dip.Ed., F.L.S.,
Curator of Birds, London Zoo

Edited by
Sue Jacquemier and Jessica Datta

Designed by
Sally Burrough

Illustrated by
Trevor Boyer, John Francis,
Robert Jefferson, Ken Lilly,
Malcolm McGregor, Robert Morton

First published in 1978 by
Usborne Publishing Ltd.,
20 Garrick Street,
London WC2E 9BJ

Introduction

We share our world with many other animals, and of these, I find birds the most fascinating.

This book shows you some of the most interesting and unusual birds and explains their amazing behaviour. It covers all the main groups of birds, from Ostriches to Birds of Paradise, and tells you where they live, what they eat, how they bring up their young, and how they escape from their enemies.

Many of the birds shown in this book are now rare, or even on the verge of extinction, because the places in which they live and their food supplies have been destroyed. People clear forests and drain land for farming, build cities and roads, and pollute the sea, often without thought for the wildlife they damage.

Birds need our protection. I hope that you enjoy this book and that it will help to show you the importance of conserving our bird life.

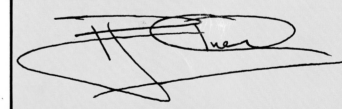

Peter Olney
London Zoo

Birds on the front cover:

1. Scarlet Ibis
2. Monkey-eating Eagle
3. Woodcock
4. Shelduck
5. House Martin
6. Bee Hummingbird
7. Marabou Stork
8. Cassowary
9. Great Bustard
10. Emperor Penguin and chick
11. Yellow-headed Amazon Parrot
12. Crowned Crane
13. Eagle Owl
14. Great Crested Grebe
15. Tufted Puffin
16. Lady Amherst's Pheasant

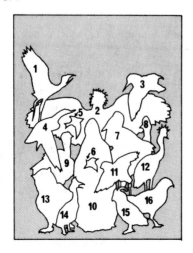

These birds are not
drawn to scale

2

Topaz
Hummingbird

Hyacinthine
Macaw

Cock of
the Rock

All these birds live in the jungles
of South America.

HOW BIRDS LIVE

Tony Bremner

Contents

How Birds Live

The First Birds

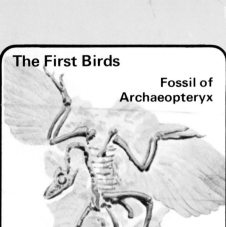

Fossil of Archaeopteryx

Birds are the only animals that have feathers. They have been on earth for millions of years, long before there were any people. Birds are said to have developed from flying reptiles, and the earliest known bird is Archaeopteryx. It was discovered in Germany as a fossil, and we know it was a bird because you can see where the feathers were. It lived about 150 million years ago.

Birds are not the only animals that can fly: bats are flying mammals, and nearly all insects fly at some time in their lives.

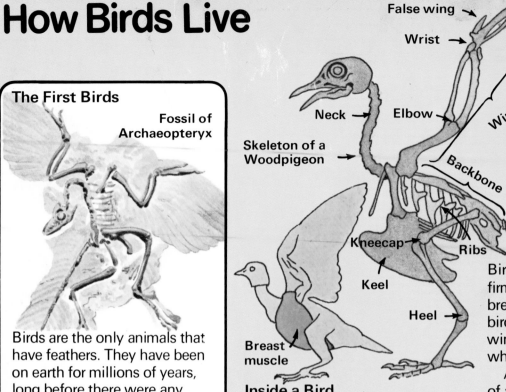

Skeleton of a Woodpigeon

False wing
Wrist
Neck
Elbow
Wing
Backbone
Tail
Lung
Air sacs
Kneecap
Keel
Ribs
Heel
Breast muscle

Inside a Bird

Birds have many hollow bones and these keep them light in the air. The bones are strong, because they have lots of slender struts inside them which criss-cross the hollow spaces. These act rather like the girders which hold up a building.

Birds have powerful muscles firmly anchored between a large breast bone and each wing. When birds fly, these muscles pull the wings down. The wings go up when the muscles relax.

A bird needs to breathe in a lot of air when it is flying, so it has extra sacs or bags for air, as well as lungs. These also help to keep the bird light.

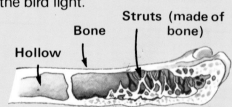

Hollow
Bone
Struts (made of bone)

The parts inside a bird that digest and break up food are similar to ours. The food passes from the mouth down a tube into the crop (see the drawing below). The crop in many birds is mainly a storage bag and some birds bring up food for their young from the crop.

The food then passes to the first part of the stomach where it mixes with digestive juices.

Birds have no teeth, so most of the "chewing" is done in the second part of the stomach, or gizzard, where it is ground to a pulp. Some birds swallow pebbles or grit to help this grinding process in the gizzard.

The digested food then goes down the intestine, and its goodness passes through the wall of the intestine into the blood. The waste passes to the cloaca and out of the body.

Beaks and Eating

Birds' beaks are specially suited to the ways they feed. Here are some examples of different types of beak.

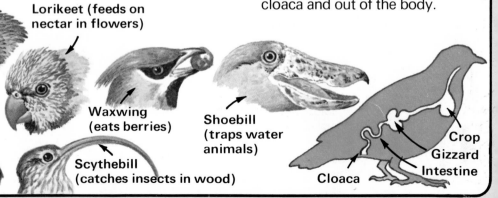

Saddlebill (stabs water animals)

Lorikeet (feeds on nectar in flowers)

Eagle (tears flesh)

Waxwing (eats berries)

Shoebill (traps water animals)

Bee-eater (catches bees and other insects)

Scythebill (catches insects in wood)

Cloaca

Crop
Gizzard
Intestine

Feathers

Shaft

Barbs

Contour feather

Down

A bird has two main types of feathers: contour feathers and down. Contour feathers cover the bird, overlapping each other, and help waterproof it. The down is usually hidden under the contour feathers, and helps keep the bird warm. All a bird's feathers together are called its plumage.

Starling in breeding plumage

Ptarmigan camouflaged against patchy snow.

Adult birds moult regularly. That is, they shed their old feathers and grow new ones. When some birds moult, they grow feathers of a different colour specially for the breeding season.

When a bird's colour blends in well with its background, it helps hide the bird from enemies. This is called camouflage.

Birds spend a lot of time keeping their feathers clean and in order. They nibble at their feathers, pulling each one through the beak. This is called preening. Birds bathe often too, in water or dust.

Treecreeper preening

Taking Off

Greylag Goose

Most birds take off by jumping into the air, but many find this difficult. Swans, Geese and some Ducks need long runways to get up enough speed to take off, rather like most aircraft. (See page 19 for a picture of Flamingos taking off.) Some birds, like Ostriches and Penguins, cannot fly at all.

In the Air

Albatross gliding

Once in the air, smaller birds, like Sparrows, flap their wings fast. Hummingbirds can hover in the air. Larger birds, like Eagles, glide and soar. Soaring birds ride up on warm air currents, and glide downwards with stiff wings. This saves energy. Some birds, like this Albatross, hardly flap their wings at all.

Landing

Herring Gull

To land, most birds glide within range of their target, then drop their feet, cup their wings, and spread their tails. This slows them down and also helps them keep their balance.

Migration

The most common kind of migration is the twice-yearly journey made by many birds between their summer and winter feeding grounds. Most migrations are by birds that live in the northern half of the world. When winter comes, they fly south, where summer is just beginning. At the end of the southern summer, they fly north again. This way they never have to suffer a harsh, cold winter, and they have a better chance of finding food.

Arctic Terns migrate from the Arctic to the Antarctic every year.

How Do Birds Know What to Do?

Many birds find food, fly, mate, rear their young and migrate over long distances without having to be taught. They do all these things by instinct. For example, it is instinct that guides all the birds of one species to build their nests in one particular way. Experiments have shown that chicks brought up separately from other birds behave exactly like other members of their species.

Birds need to repeat many of the instinctive things they do to make them perfect. Birds are also able to learn from their mistakes and by copying others. Blue Tits, for example, have learnt to peck through milk bottle tops to drink the milk. One bird discovered this way of feeding and others copied it.

The different stages in a bird's life are all ruled by instinct and learning. The pictures below explain some of these stages.

1

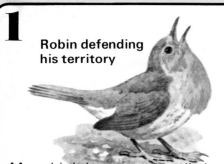

Robin defending his territory

Many birds have an area called a "territory" for the breeding season. They guard their nests from enemies and threaten other birds if they come inside the territory for food. Actual fights are quite rare.

2

Sage Grouse displaying

To attract a mate, many birds "display" to each other. The male may show off his brightly coloured plumage. Some birds fly or jump about in special ways, while others sing. Mating cannot normally happen until after this display.

3

Black-winged Stilts mating

The male climbs on the female's back to mate. He sends a liquid containing sperms into her body through an opening. Some sperms reach the eggs inside the female. When a sperm and an egg join, it is called fertilization. Only fertilized eggs can grow into chicks.

4

Little Ringed Plover on nest

Eggs laid in holes are usually white or a plain pale colour. But eggs laid on the ground must be camouflaged (see page 5) to hide them from enemies. Birds sit on their eggs to keep them warm while the

Kingfisher's egg (laid in hole)

chicks are growing. This is called incubating the eggs.

5

Egg tooth

Moorhen chick hatching

The chick has to break open the hard egg shell. It makes the first crack with the sharp egg tooth on the tip of its bill. It moves about and jerks its legs to hatch out.

6

Herring Gull chick

Wryneck chick

Birds that hatch inside the protection of a nest or hole are normally blind and naked. Those hatched on the ground can see and have some feathers. They can usually feed themselves and walk soon after hatching.

7

Dunnock

Chicks beg for food by opening their beaks, which are often brightly coloured inside, or by pecking at the parents' bills. This gives the parents a strong urge to feed the young.

The Names of Birds

Scientists have given names to different groups of animals and plants. All birds are in the **Class** of animals called Aves, which is the Latin word for birds. Scientists use Latin or Greek names so that people all over the world, whatever language they speak, will know what bird or group of birds they are talking about.

Birds are divided into 27 **Orders.** One order is called Falconiformes. In this order there are five **Families,** for example the Family Accipitridae. In this Family are Eagles, Hawks and some Vultures. They are grouped in **Genera** (singular: **Genus**), and there are 64 Genera in the family Accipitridae.

One Genus is called *Accipiter,* and it includes 47 **Species**. One of these Species is the Northern Goshawk (its Latin name is *Accipiter gentilis*).

Northern Goshawk *(Accipiter gentilis)*

Class: Aves (Birds)		
Order: Falconiformes	26 other ORDERS	
Family: Accipitridae	4 other FAMILIES	
Genus: Accipiter	63 other GENERA	
Species: Accipiter gentilis	46 other SPECIES	

What is a Species?

The Mauritius Kestrel is one of many species in danger of becoming extinct.

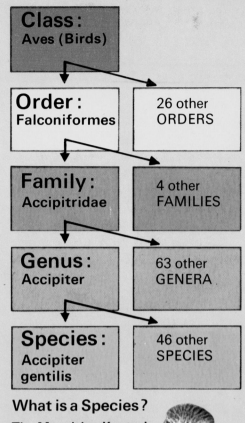

There are over 8,600 species of birds in the world. Members of the same species all look alike and behave in the same way. For example, all White Storks have red bills. Sometimes the males of a species look different from the females, but all the females look alike, and all the males look alike.

The members of a species can breed together, but members of two different species do not normally produce young.

Many species, like the bird above, are now very rare. When there are no more members of a species left, the species is said to be extinct.

Why are there Different Species?

Warbler Finch

Large Tree Finch

Cactus Ground Finch

Large Ground Finch

Darwin's Finches

The many different species of birds have developed over millions of years. The way that different birds look and act has changed very slowly. This slow process of change is called evolution.

Here is one way this can happen: imagine a group of seed-eating birds living in a particular area. One day, just by chance, one chick hatches which has a slightly stronger beak than the rest. This means that it can eat hard seeds that the others cannot break. It thrives and breeds, and some of its young are born with the same strong beak. Gradually the birds with strong beaks grow in numbers and a new species evolves. This new species eats different food from the first species, so there is still enough food to go round.

Any accidental change may start a new chain of evolution —longer legs or brighter colours, for example. But the change will only be passed on if it helps the animal to survive. Most accidental changes are not helpful, and the animal dies without passing on the new feature.

A great naturalist called Charles Darwin confirmed this pattern of evolution when he studied Finches in the Galapagos Islands in 1835. The pictures above show some of the species that he realized had developed from one original species.

Ostriches

Ostriches and their relatives cannot fly, but, apart from the Kiwi, they have long strong legs and can run fast. Their soft plumes are more like hair than feathers.

Male

Female

Ostriches can be three metres high and can weigh 140 kilos.

Their good eyesight and height help them to spot enemies, like lions, hyenas and jackals, before it is too late to run away.

Male Ostriches were killed for the white plumes in their tails and wings.

They use their strong legs to kick their enemies.

Ostriches have only two toes on each foot.

Ostriches are the tallest and heaviest of all birds. They live in Africa on grass or scrubland, where they move about in flocks of about twelve birds, sometimes with herds of zebra or wildebeest. They feed on leaves, berries, seeds and small animals like locusts or mice, and also swallow pebbles to help grind up their food. They drink a lot of water and eat juicy plants, like cacti, which contain water. Adult Ostriches can run up to 56 kph.

8

1 How Ostriches Breed

The male Ostrich mates with two or three females. He performs a mating dance to attract them. He waves his head and neck around and shows off his plumes.

2

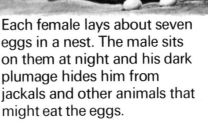

Each female lays about seven eggs in a nest. The male sits on them at night and his dark plumage hides him from jackals and other animals that might eat the eggs.

3

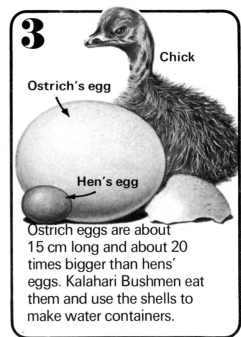

Chick

Ostrich's egg

Hen's egg

Ostrich eggs are about 15 cm long and about 20 times bigger than hens' eggs. Kalahari Bushmen eat them and use the shells to make water containers.

4

Almost immediately after hatching, the chicks are able to run about. When they are frightened, they lie flat on the ground where they are well camouflaged.

Other Flightless Birds

Cassowary

Cassowaries live in rain forests in Northern Australia and New Guinea. Their strange horn and spiky feathers protect them as they move through the jungle.

Emu and chick

The Australian Emu lives on grasslands and eats leaves, seeds and insects. The male sits on the eggs, which are green. These hatch into stripy chicks.

Plumes

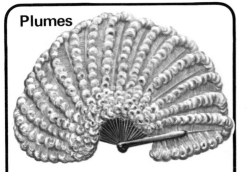

In the 19th century, Ostriches nearly became extinct. Millions were killed for their plumes, which were used to decorate hats and to make fans like this one.

Rhea

The Rhea of South America has a dull grey plumage. Several females lay their eggs in the same nest. The male Rhea incubates them and looks after the chicks.

Kiwi

The Kiwi of New Zealand's forests is nocturnal (active at night). Its nostrils at the tip of its beak help it to smell berries, worms and insects, which it eats.

Penguins

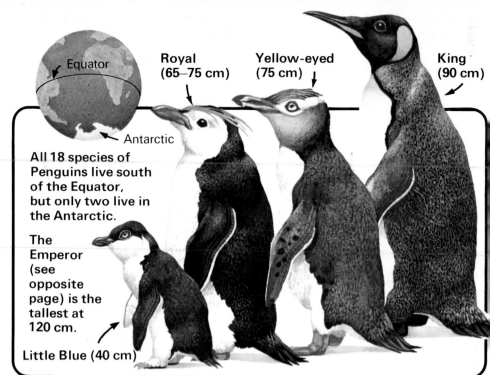

Penguins cannot fly, and their short legs make them clumsy on land. When they have to move fast, they toboggan on their bellies. But Penguins can swim faster than any other birds.

All Penguins live by the sea in large groups, called rookeries. They catch fish and squid to eat.

They can live 25–30 years, but sea lions and whales hunt them and Skuas swoop down to attack their chicks.

Equator

Antarctic

Royal (65–75 cm)

Yellow-eyed (75 cm)

King (90 cm)

All 18 species of Penguins live south of the Equator, but only two live in the Antarctic.

The Emperor (see opposite page) is the tallest at 120 cm.

Little Blue (40 cm)

Keeping Warm

Jackass Penguin

Penguins have oily, thickly-packed feathers which keep heat in and water out. If they get too hot they fluff up their feathers and hold out their wings.

Rockhopper Penguins

Rockhoppers are small, noisy and playful. They do not live on ice, but on rocky coastlines.

Their name comes from their skill in hopping from ledge to ledge.

They make nests in clumps of grass between rocks or in caves.

They use their sharp claws and hooked bills to help them climb up the rocks.

Pairs of Rockhoppers greet each other by lifting their bills and squawking.

1 Emperor Penguins

In winter, Emperors waddle in single file to the nesting grounds inland. They are fat from eating all summer at sea. The fat layer under their skin protects them from the cold.

2

Each year the same pair meet and mate. The female lays a single egg on the ice. Then she travels many miles to feed at sea. The male stays to care for the egg.

3

He keeps the egg warm by putting it on his feet and covering it with his loose belly skin. The egg is completely hidden. The male hardly moves and does not eat while the female is away.

4

In eight weeks the egg hatches. The mother returns and looks after the young. The chick crouches on its mother's feet. The hungry father, now half his normal weight, goes off to feed.

5

The parents take turns to go and hunt for food. They feed the chick by regurgitating, or bringing up, partly digested fish from their crops.

6

The older chicks huddle together to keep warm while their parents are feeding. Parents and chicks go back to the sea in the summer.

Swimming and Jumping

Penguins' bodies are streamlined like torpedos. They "fly" through the water using their wings as flippers. They can shoot out of the water on to land in one leap.

Gentoo Penguins

Grebes and Divers

Grebes and Divers are water birds. They have streamlined bodies, long necks and sharp beaks. They dive for fish and small water animals.

Their legs are set far back, so they swim well but walk with difficulty.

Different species of Grebes are found all over the world, often on inland waters. Divers, or Loons, live mainly on northern seas, normally coming inland only to breed.

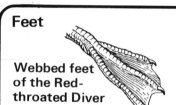

Feet

Webbed feet of the Red-throated Diver

Toes of the Great Crested Grebe

Flaps of skin open and push away water.

Flaps of skin fold up to let water flow between toes.

Divers have webbed feet, but Grebes do not. Both use only their feet for swimming under the water, and not their wings as Penguins do. Grebes have separate toes with flaps of skin between them. These flaps fold up against the toes when they draw the feet up for the next stroke, or when they dive. This allows the water to pass between the toes easily.

Great Crested Grebes

Non-breeding plumage

Breeding plumage

The dance often starts and ends with a bout of head-shaking. The pair face each other and waggle their heads from side to side.

Here a Grebe is crouching low in the water, with its wings spread and its chest puffed out.

1 The Dance

In the breeding season, the Great Crested Grebe grows a dark brown frill of feathers round its neck, and two black ear tufts. When two Grebes meet, they often get very excited, and they spread out these frills and tufts like a ruff.

Great Crested Grebes are well known for their courtship dance, which includes many different positions and actions. Three of them are shown here: crouching, head-shaking and diving for weeds. The dance means that two

birds have paired up, and will probably mate. It is also performed by Grebes at other times. Some of the positions are used as signals or warnings to rival birds.

Black-throated Divers

The Black-throated Diver cannot walk very well. It has to drag its body on land, so it builds its nest near the bank. It shuffles down a runway made of flattened grass into the water.

Great Northern Divers

Breeding plumage

Non-breeding plumage

Birds often have much brighter coloured plumage in the breeding season, and Great Northern Divers become a completely different colour. This special breeding plumage can help birds attract a mate. The rest of the year, there is no need for their colours to be so striking, so they become more drab and dull. This helps them to avoid their enemies.

Sometimes a pair will dive to the bottom and pull up some weed. When they surface they swim towards each other. They may rise out of the water, paddling hard with their feet to stay up. When they meet they bring their chests almost together and offer the weed to each other.

2 Nest-building

The birds lay their eggs on a floating platform, made of piled-up weed and sticks. They trample the weed to make a solid nest and wall it up round the edge to make a hollow in the centre for the eggs.

3 Chicks

The striped chicks can swim as soon as they hatch. But often they prefer to be carried on the parents' backs. The parents feed them on insects and small fish. They do not begin to dive for food until they are six weeks old.

Pelicans and Cormorants

Pelicans and Cormorants are fishing birds and usually live in colonies, or large groups. They are found all over the world on both freshwater lakes and sea coasts. Although they fly well, their short stumpy legs make them move slowly on land. After diving for fish, Cormorants stand with their wings spread out to dry.

The other birds on these pages belong to the same Order, or group, as Pelicans and Cormorants.

White Pelicans

White Pelicans fly and fish together. They glide over lakes with their huge wings, and use their great bills to scoop up fish. The bill pouch can hold 13 litres of water. Sometimes Pelicans form a horseshoe-shaped line and swim towards each other, joining up to make a circle. Then they dip their beaks at exactly the same time to catch as many trapped fish as possible. Adult Pelicans can catch nine kilos of fish a day.

1

Brown Pelicans

These sea birds are the smallest Pelicans. They dive-bomb into the water and catch fish in their pouches.

2

The Pelicans surface and then swallow the fish whole. Gulls gather round fishing Pelicans hoping to steal some of the catch.

3

Adult Pelicans bring up fish they have swallowed to feed to their young. The chicks put their heads right inside their parents' beak pouches.

1 Shags

Shags nest in crowded colonies on rocky cliffs. Their nests are made out of twigs and seaweed.

2

The female lays about three eggs and the parents take turns to sit on them until they hatch.

3

Chicks

The chicks are born naked. After a few days they begin to grow dark brown downy feathers and open their eyes. After seven weeks they have learnt to fly.

Guano Islands

There is a group of islands off the coast of South America where thousands of Guanay Cormorants live. The ground is covered with deep layers of the birds' droppings. This is called guano, and it is rich in a chemical called nitrate. People collect the guano and use it as a fertilizer for farmland.

Frigate Bird

Frigate Birds live on coasts and islands. The male has a bright red patch of loose skin under his beak. He can blow it up like a balloon to attract females.

Gannets and Boobies

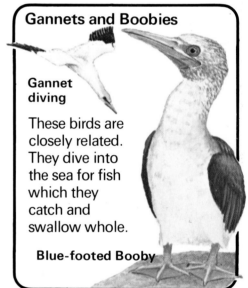

Gannet diving

These birds are closely related. They dive into the sea for fish which they catch and swallow whole.

Blue-footed Booby

Snake Bird

The Anhinga is called the Snake Bird because it moves its head and neck above the water in an S shape. It stabs fish with its sharp beak, tosses them into the air and then catches and swallows them. The Anhinga also eats frogs, newts, salamanders and crayfish.

Storks and Herons

Storks and Herons belong to the same group as Flamingos (see page 18), Ibises and Spoonbills. All these birds have long legs, large wings and a short tail. Most of them feed in shallow water and marshes. They nest in colonies.

White Storks

Storks make a clattering noise when they meet. They throw back their heads and clap the two halves of their bills together fast.

White Storks often nest on house roofs or chimneys. In Holland, people put up poles with a cartwheel laid flat on top for Storks to build on.

The Migration of the White Storks

EUROPE
Istanbul
Gibraltar
AFRICA

→ Routes taken by White Storks in late summer

Most White Storks leaving Europe cross the sea to Africa at one of its narrowest points (Gibraltar or Istanbul). They avoid long sea crossings because there are no currents of hot air over the water for them to glide on. They mostly glide and soar and only occasionally flap their wings.

At the end of the summer, both adults and young leave the nest and migrate to a warmer place.

The nest is built of sticks, paper, rubbish and often horse manure. The Storks often go back to last year's nest. They repair it, so it grows bigger every year.

Eight chicks may hatch, but those hatched last often do not get enough food to live. The adults feed the chicks on chewed-up mice, frogs and other small animals.

White Storks breed in Europe, Central Asia and North Africa. Hundreds of them used to migrate from Africa to Europe in early spring each year, and people would welcome them as bringers of good luck. But there are fewer and fewer White Storks nesting in places where they were once regular visitors.

Nowadays they have to face many dangers—factory chimneys, high power lines, hunters and aeroplanes. There are a few White Storks left in Asia, and in eastern Europe they still nest in large numbers. But in Japan, where they once lived, they are now extinct.

16

Grey Herons

Grey Heron in nest with young

Grey Heron in flight

Herons can be recognized by the curve in their necks when they fly. The Grey Heron eats fish, frogs and small mammals. It nests in trees.

Black Herons

The Black Heron can make an umbrella shape with its wings, which shades the surface of the water from the bright African sun. This helps the bird to catch fish, perhaps because it can then see them more clearly.

Egrets

Hat decorated with Egret feathers

Male Egrets were hunted for these long back feathers.

Egrets are closely related to Herons. In the 1900's thousands of Egrets were killed for their fine feathers. These were used to decorate fashionable hats.

Great White Egret (or Great White Heron)

Ibises

Scarlet Ibis

Ibises use their curved bills to probe for and catch prey. The Scarlet Ibis lives in rain forests in South America.

Marabou Storks

The Marabou has a fleshy bag under its beak. Like Vultures, Marabous eat dead flesh left by lions and other hunters.

Spoonbills

Roseate Spoonbill

The Spoonbill wades in shallow water, moving its spoon-shaped bill from side to side. It traps small fish and animals as water flows through its bill.

Sacred Ibis

The ancient Egyptians thought the Sacred Ibis was a god who had come back to life as a bird. It is now extinct in Egypt but lives in other parts of Africa.

Flamingos

There are several different species of Flamingos. The ones shown here are Greater Flamingos. They live in large groups in places where the water is shallow and salty. Compared with the size of their bodies, their necks and legs are longer than those of any other birds.

Flamingos are so big that they need a lot of space to take off into the air. It is hard for one bird to take off alone because its neighbours are crowded too close. The whole flock usually flies off together.

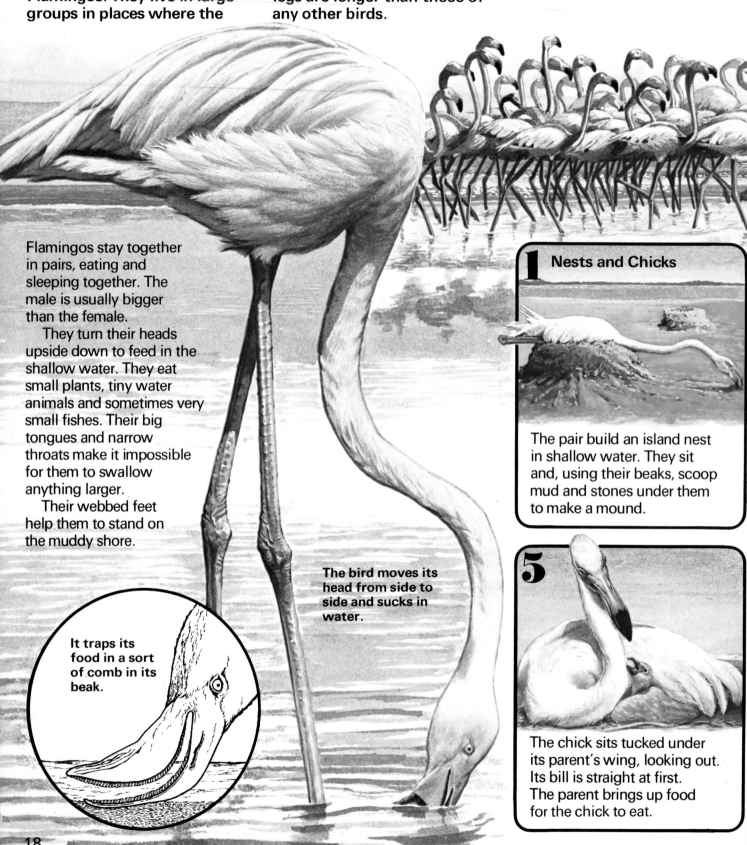

Flamingos stay together in pairs, eating and sleeping together. The male is usually bigger than the female.

They turn their heads upside down to feed in the shallow water. They eat small plants, tiny water animals and sometimes very small fishes. Their big tongues and narrow throats make it impossible for them to swallow anything larger.

Their webbed feet help them to stand on the muddy shore.

It traps its food in a sort of comb in its beak.

The bird moves its head from side to side and sucks in water.

1 Nests and Chicks

The pair build an island nest in shallow water. They sit and, using their beaks, scoop mud and stones under them to make a mound.

5

The chick sits tucked under its parent's wing, looking out. Its bill is straight at first. The parent brings up food for the chick to eat.

Flocks are easily frightened away by low-flying aeroplanes. Unfortunately, airports are often built near the flat areas where Flamingos live. Colonies are sometimes completely deserted because of this disturbance.

Flamingos fly in long lines with their necks and legs stretched out straight. They make honking noises as they fly.

2

The birds make a hollow in the top of the mound and the female usually lays one egg. The hollow stops it from rolling out of the nest.

3

The adult Flamingos take it in turns to sit on the egg. They fold their long legs under their bodies while sitting on the nest.

4

When it rains, the Flamingo spreads its wings to stop the mud nest from being washed away. After about a month, the chick hatches.

6

At first the chick is grey. The pink colour comes later from a natural chemical in its food. Scarlet Ibises also get their colour from their food.

7

When the young leave the nest they form flocks of their own, but their parents still feed them for some time. Slowly the chicks' bills grow and they begin to feed themselves.

Swans

Swans are large birds that live on and by ponds, lakes and rivers. They have stout legs and webbed feet so they swim well, but they waddle on land.

They eat mostly water plants and use their long necks to reach down for food. Most Swans live in flocks, except in the breeding season when they make pairs.

When Mute Swans fly, their wing beats make a loud creaking noise.

The cob guards the nest and will attack another Swan that comes too close.

The nest is built of grasses and rushes on raised ground, though it is usually surrounded by water.

Whooper Swan

Trumpeter Swan

Because they are so heavy, Swans need a long run across the water before taking off.

Bewick's Swan

There are eight kinds of Swans. The male is called a cob, the female a pen, and the young are called cygnets.

This Swan is looking for food on the water bed.

This Swan is preening its feathers.

Cygnets are often carried on their parents' backs.

Mute Swan

Black Swans

Black Swans of Australia gather in huge flocks. They have white wing feathers which can only be seen when they fly.

Geese

Geese are strong, stocky birds that feed on grasses, grain and other plants. They live in flocks called gaggles. Although they have webbed feet, they spend most of their time on land, usually near rivers and lakes. The female is called a goose, the male a gander and the chicks goslings.

Geese have been kept for food for thousands of years and were popular with the Romans, Greeks and Egyptians in ancient times.

Néné or Hawaiian Goose

Red-breasted Goose

Canada Goose

Snow Goose

Domestic Geese

Geese are easy to fatten because they eat a lot. Their down is used to stuff pillows and their wing feathers were once made into quill pens.

Greylag Geese

In early spring, a goose follows a gander about, watching him out of the corner of her eye. He gets very excited.

The gander rushes to attack any other young ganders in the gaggle. He honks loudly and beats his wings.

When they back away, he hurries back to his mate calling triumphantly. He impresses her by this show of strength.

Together they dip their necks, lowering and pointing their heads. This means they are getting to know each other better before mating.

Like all birds, Geese have no language. But they make noises, and can also "talk" to each other with positions and movements of the body.

Imprinting

When goslings hatch they become attached to the first large moving object they see. This is called "imprinting". Goslings hatched by hens, or even by people, accept them as "mother" and follow them everywhere.

Ducks

Ducks, like Swans and Geese, are waterfowl. They can be recognized by their flattened bill, short legs and webbed feet. They have thick waterproof feathers covering a layer of down which keeps them warm. Ducks have been domesticated and eaten for centuries and they are still hunted for sport.

Male and female Ducks, unlike most Geese and Swans, look different—the male, called a drake, is usually more colourful than the female, called a duck. Most Ducks nest near the water's edge.

Shelduck

Goosander ducklings can swim as soon as they get into the water for the first time. The eggs are often laid in holes high up in trees. After hatching, the young jump out. They are so light that they do not hurt themselves.

The Shoveler has a broad, shovel-like beak. Like the Flamingo, it has a sort of comb in its beak which strains very tiny water animals out of the water. Shovelers often feed closely together because groups stir up more food in the water.

Shoveler duck

Goosander duck

Mandarin drake

Shoveler drake

Ducks use oil from a gland near their tails to keep their feathers in good order. They spread the oil all over themselves with their beaks.

Feeding

Pintail up-ending

Gadwall dabbling

Pochard diving

Wigeon grazing

Some Ducks feed on or just under the water. They eat small plants and animals by sucking up water and sieving the food through their beaks. They can also up-end, or tip up, to reach down further.

Diving Ducks can dive down to the water bed to feed on plants and small creatures. They can stay under the water for half a minute or more before bobbing up to the surface.

Wigeon graze on grasses and other plants on salt marshes near sea coasts. Wigeon that live in the far north also eat berries from bushes.

In the winter many Shelduck fly south to warmer areas. Those in Scandinavia fly as far as the Mediterranean, and those in northern Asia fly to India, Pakistan and Burma.

When Ducks land on water they put out their feet to act as brakes.

Mallard drakes

Mallard duck

Goosander drake

This Duck is asleep with its head under its wing. In winter it keeps its nostrils warm like this. It stands on one leg and warms the other leg against its body.

Goldeneye duck

Tufted drake

Goldeneye drake

The Goldeneye displays in the water when he has chosen a mate. He throws his head back and splashes with his feet.

Nesting

Eider Duck

Eider Ducks live near northern seas. They nest in colonies. The nest is a hollow in the ground and the female plucks down from her breast to line it. When the ducklings have left, people collect the down to fill eiderdowns and duvets.

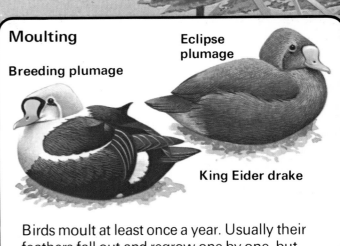

Moulting

Eclipse plumage

Breeding plumage

King Eider drake

Birds moult at least once a year. Usually their feathers fall out and regrow one by one, but Ducks lose their flight feathers all at once and so they cannot fly. The drake's feathers during the flightless period are dull and help hide him. Later he moults this "eclipse plumage".

23

Birds of Prey

Birds of prey are hunters and feed on other birds, small mammals, snakes, fish and insects. Their eyesight is much better than ours and they have powerful wings and strong hooked beaks. The largest bird of prey is the Andean Condor, which has a wingspan of three metres. The Pygmy Falconet is the smallest and is only 16 cm long.

Condors can soar to a tremendous height on their enormous wings. They ride on a rising current of warm air called a thermal.

Eagles can kill animals three times their own weight, but usually their prey is much smaller.

The Golden Eagle builds its nest, called an eyrie, on a rocky crag or in a very tall tree. Every year the pair return to the same nest and add to it. It can be as large as two metres across. Sometimes the nest becomes so heavy that it falls out of the tree.

Condors, like Vultures, do not kill their prey, but eat only carrion, or dead flesh.

Californian Condors are very rare birds. Cattle farmers poison dead animals to kill scavengers, like wolves and coyotes. Sometimes Condors eat the poisoned bait and die. Many others have been shot or have been unable to find food, because the cattle ranches in the area where they live have been changed into fruit farms. The few Condors left alive are now guarded in a reserve.

1 African Fish Eagles

Before they mate, African Fish Eagles display together in the air. A male and a female link claws and tumble through the air, whirling round and round in cartwheels.

2

Chicks

They return to last year's stick nest high in a tree, and add to it. The female lays two or three eggs and incubates them. The parents feed the young with fish or sometimes small water birds.

3

When their feathers have grown, the eaglets exercise their wings. They rush about the nest flapping them. After ten weeks the eaglets are strong enough to make their first flight.

Eaglet

Feeding

Vultures

Flocks of Vultures feed on the remains of prey left by other animals. Their featherless heads do not get sticky with blood.

Ospreys

The Osprey hunts for fish. It circles above the water and dives feet first when it spots one. It plunges in and seizes the fish in its claws.

Falconry

Peregrine Falcon

Pheasant

Secretary Birds

These birds kill snakes by stamping on them, jumping back, and stamping again. Their crests look like quill pens behind a secretary's ear.

Kites

Kites are scavengers and often live near towns. They turn and swoop in the air and then drop down to pick up scraps from the street.

Hood

Falcons and Hawks can be trained for hunting in a sport called falconry. Falconers cover the birds' heads with hoods to calm them. Some Falcons can dive at up to 320 kph, which makes them superb hunters for Partridges and Pheasants.

Pheasants, Grouse and Chickens

All these birds belong to the group that includes the domestic chicken, the most common bird in the world. The group also includes one of the rarest—the Imperial Pheasant. People hunt many of these species.

The cock has sharp spurs, which he uses when fighting rivals.

The Yokohama chicken has been bred for its long tail feathers.

Domestic chickens like this Ross Brown can lay an egg a day.

The Silver Sebright is a breed of domestic chicken.

Turkeys

Female

The male puffs out his chest to attract a female.

Wild Turkeys first lived in America and were brought back to Europe by explorers. In the wild they live in woods and eat nuts, acorns, berries and insects. At night they roost (or sleep) in trees.

There are many kinds of domestic chickens, but they have all been bred from the same species—the Red Jungle Fowl of South-East Asia. It looks like a farmyard cockerel, but has much shinier feathers. It still lives in forests and jungles where it makes its nest out of dry leaves and grass. Like many other birds, it breeds once a year.

Black Grouse

Male

The female is called a Greyhen, although her feathers are brown and help hide her when she is sitting on the nest.

The displaying Blackcocks fan out their tails and make a "roocooing" call.

The adult male is called a Blackcock. His tail normally looks like this.

Black Grouse live on the edges of forests and on moors. The males have a special area of ground, called a lek, where 10—30 of them gather at the beginning of spring. There each Blackcock displays his feathers, hisses, crows and puffs out his chest as a challenge to other males. As the females arrive at the edge of the lek they are attracted by the males' display. Then they mate.

Pheasants

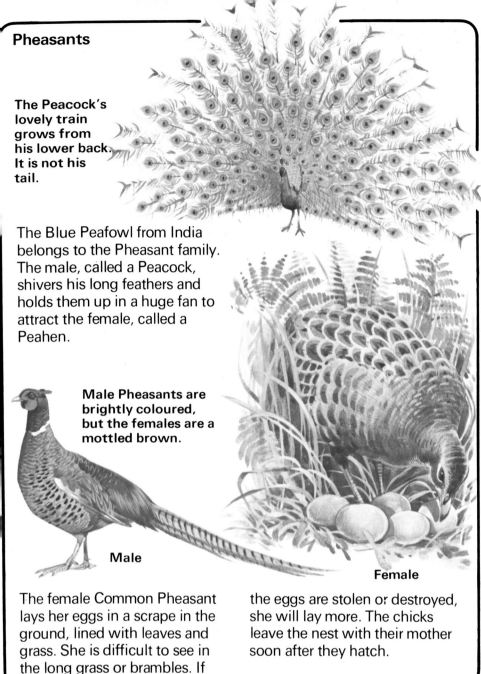

The Peacock's lovely train grows from his lower back. It is not his tail.

The Blue Peafowl from India belongs to the Pheasant family. The male, called a Peacock, shivers his long feathers and holds them up in a huge fan to attract the female, called a Peahen.

Male Pheasants are brightly coloured, but the females are a mottled brown.

Male

Female

The female Common Pheasant lays her eggs in a scrape in the ground, lined with leaves and grass. She is difficult to see in the long grass or brambles. If the eggs are stolen or destroyed, she will lay more. The chicks leave the nest with their mother soon after they hatch.

Partridges

Red-legged Partridges live on farmland, rocky mountain sides, and scrubland. If you disturb a covey, or group, of Partridges, they will all fly off together, beating their wings noisily.

They nest in hollows scraped in the ground and lined with dead leaves and grass. After hatching, the chicks stay close to their mother, and at night shelter for warmth under her wings.

1 Mallee Fowl

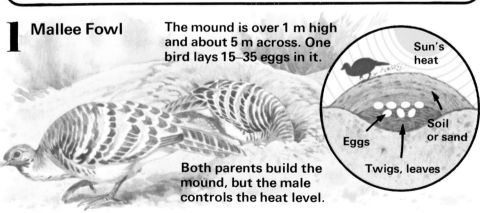

The mound is over 1 m high and about 5 m across. One bird lays 15—35 eggs in it.

Sun's heat

Eggs

Soil or sand

Twigs, leaves

Both parents build the mound, but the male controls the heat level.

2

The chicks have to struggle out from the egg chamber in the centre of the mound.

Instead of sitting on its eggs to incubate them, the Mallee Fowl of Australia lays them inside a huge mound made some weeks before from twigs, leaves and soil or sand. The leaves rot and make the mound warm, just like a compost heap. The Mallee Fowl keeps the temperature just right. If it is too hot during the day, it piles on more earth to keep out the sun's rays. In the evening it scrapes the earth off to let the heat escape. It tests the temperature by pushing its beak into the mound.

Waders

Most Waders are birds of the shore. Many have long legs and wade without getting their feathers wet. In the summer, many fly from Africa to breed in Europe, where there is usually plenty to eat and to feed the young.

Most Waders make their nests on the ground on beaches or pasture land. The speckled eggs are difficult for enemies to spot among the pebbles or grasses.

Phalaropes

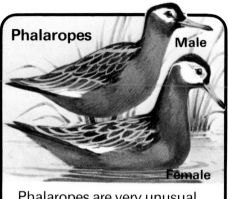

Male

Female

Phalaropes are very unusual. The female is more colourful than the male and she displays to attract him. The male sits on the eggs and looks after the chicks.

Woodcocks

The Woodcock's plumage is mottled brown, grey and black. When it sits on the ground surrounded by dead leaves, it is almost invisible to enemies.

Dotterels

This Dotterel is leading the fox away from her nest. She pretends to be injured and drags her wing so that the fox follows her. If the fox pounces, she will fly away.

All birds have beaks which have become adapted to finding and eating particular foods. Birds that live in the same area often eat different foods, so there is enough to go round.

All the birds in this picture are in their summer plumage.

Redshanks make quick pecks in the mud to eat small shrimps, snails and worms. Their prey is small so they need to eat a lot and may feed on moonlit nights as well as in the daytime.

Dunlin eat worms and shrimps. They make quick little jabs in the mud with their beaks. This is called "stitching" because the rows of little holes look like sewing stitches.

Oystercatchers use their strong bills to prise open cockle and mussel shells, and to hammer at shells to break them.

Curlews live on mudflats and pasture land. They probe for food in the mud with their curved bills. They pull out worms and other small animals.

Ruff in normal plumage →

Ruffs

Reeve

Ruff in breeding plumage

The male Ruff gets his name from the ruff of feathers he grows to attract the female. Like Blackcocks, Ruffs display in groups on a lek. The female is called a Reeve.

Cranes

Cranes are tall birds with long legs and long necks. There are 14 species and most live near marshes or rivers. They eat grain, berries and other plants as well as frogs, small reptiles and mice. They live in large flocks, except in the breeding season when they make pairs. They fly with their necks and legs stretched out straight.

Crowned Cranes live in Africa. They are noisy birds and shriek when they fly. They feed in marshes and stamp their feet to disturb frogs, which they stab with their beaks.

Pairs of Cranes put their beaks in the air and call together.

Before mating, Cranes perform an exciting dance. These Sarus Cranes stretch up and bow down, leap about and flap their wings.

Knots migrate north in autumn. In winter vast flocks gather to feed in estuaries.

Turnstones turn over stones and pull apart seaweed looking for small crabs and sandhoppers.

Dunlin

Turnstones

Snipe push their bills deep in the mud and swallow worms and insects whole.

Avocets stand in shallow water to feed. They sweep their upward-curved bills from side to side, sifting insects and shellfish out of the water.

Gulls, Terns and Auks

Most seabirds are basically black, white or a mixture of both. They have webbed feet and strong bodies, and they fly well. Many have harsh, squawky voices.

The groups shown on these pages behave in different ways. Auks, such as Puffins and Guillemots, dive and swim under the water to catch their food, while Gulls and Terns feed mainly from the surface. Many Gulls scavenge inland for food as well.

Puffins

A Puffin can carry as many as 20 fish in its beak.

Puffins use their feet as rudders when landing and changing direction.

When Puffins meet, they shake their bills to greet one another.

Puffins make a burrow for their single egg in grassy places or under rocks, often in the soft soil on the top of cliffs. They dig with their beaks and use their clawed feet as shovels. Sometimes they chase out rabbits and nest in their burrows. The parents bring beakfuls of fish to their chick, which stays in the burrow until it is about six weeks old.

1 Gulls

Before mating, male and female Black-headed Gulls run side by side with their heads down.

The male also coughs up some food for the female to eat.

Gulls usually breed with the same mate for life. Every year they return in large groups to the same breeding ground. Males and females perform a courtship dance together when they are ready to mate. They gather straw, moss and bits of paper, trampling it down to make a nest.

2

Black-headed Gull with chick

Herring Gull with chick

Gulls lay up to three eggs. The parents take it in turns to sit on them and to guard against rats, foxes, dogs and other birds which might steal the eggs.

When the chicks have hatched, they beg for food from their parents. Some Gull chicks do this by cheeping and pecking at a red spot on the parent's bill.

3

Three-week-old Black-headed Gull chicks

Juvenile Black-headed Gull

Adult Black-headed Gull in breeding plumage (summer)

In winter, Black-headed Gulls have white heads with a dark blotch behind the eye.

Young Gulls learn to fly when they are about six weeks old. Until they are mature (old enough to breed), their plumage is different from the adults'. They live in the same Gull colony as their parents.

Terns

The spotted eggs are difficult to see among the pebbles and broken shells on the beach.

A male Little Tern offering food to a female.

The chicks are also well camouflaged.

Terns are sometimes called Sea Swallows because of their pointed wings and forked tails. They usually nest in large colonies, but the Little Tern prefers smaller groups. The nest is just a hollow scraped in the sand or shingle. The male courts the female with gifts of fish, which he feeds to her. After mating with him, she lays two or three eggs.

Fairy Terns

The Fairy Tern breeds on islands. It builds no nest. The female lays her eggs on a bare branch or ledge. The chicks have large feet which help them cling to the branch.

Cliff Colonies

Many seabirds live in large groups, sometimes of a thousand or more birds. They build their nests on rocks, cliffs and islands, just out of pecking distance of each other. Each bird keeps its neighbours away by stretching out its neck and aiming blows at them with its beak.

Kittiwakes build nests of seaweed, grass and mud on narrow ledges where they are safe from enemies.

Gulls, like birds of prey, can soar upwards in circles. They ride on currents of air that rise up near cliffs.

Guillemots lay their eggs on bare rock ledges. The eggs are pointed at one end, and this pear shape stops them from rolling off the ledge. If they are touched, they just roll round in a circle.

Herring Gulls are often seen inland, and some hardly ever go near the sea. They find plenty of food in cities and on farmland.

Razorbills rear their single chick in gaps between the rocks on cliff faces. They do not build any kind of nest.

Great Black-backed Gulls kill and eat Puffins, rabbits and the chicks of other birds, as well as fish.

31

Pigeons

Pigeons are found all over the world, except where it is very cold. They are rounded birds with short legs and soft feathers. There are nearly 300 species of Pigeons. Some are also called Doves, although it means the same thing.

Most Pigeons live on seeds and fruits. All of them can suck up water with their beaks, unlike other birds that have to tilt their heads back to drink.

Rock Doves

Racing Pigeons

Message tied to leg ↓

All domestic Pigeons have developed from the wild Rock Dove, which lives on cliffs and ledges. The female builds a shallow twig nest in a dark cave.

For centuries people have kept Pigeons and built dovecots for them. As Pigeons almost always find their way home they were used to carry messages. People still breed them for racing.

Dodos

The Dodo was a flightless bird related to Pigeons. Settlers on the island of Mauritius killed Dodos for food and by 1681 there were none left alive.

Show Pigeons

Kormoner

Fantail

Some Pigeons are specially bred as show birds. Sometimes their shapes are changed so much that they cannot feed their young.

City Pigeons

Most city Pigeons are descended from domestic Pigeons that have escaped or been released. They nest on ledges on buildings and eat what they find or are fed in streets and parks. They can be black, grey, brown, white, or a mixture of colours.

1 Woodpigeons

2

3

Woodpigeons live on farmland. The male puffs up the shimmery purple and green feathers on his neck to attract a female.

The male croons and the pair nibble each other's feathers and caress. Then they are ready to mate. Together they build a stick nest where the female lays two white eggs.

Birds have a bag in their gullet called a crop (see page 4). Pigeons make a type of milk in the crop and bring it up to feed to their chicks.

Cuckoos

Some members of the Cuckoo family are called parasites because the female lays her eggs in other birds' nests. Every spring, the Common Cuckoo lays about twelve eggs, each in a different nest. The bird in whose nest she leaves the egg is called the host. The host is usually a small bird, like a Warbler or a Dunnock.

Some other birds are parasitic, like the Honeyguides, the Cowbirds and the Black-headed Duck.

Female Cuckoo

The Common Cuckoo watches the Reed Warbler's nest until it is unguarded. Then she takes out one of the eggs, swallows or drops it, and lays one of her own.

Cuckoo's egg

The Cuckoo's egg is larger than the Reed Warbler's, but it is nearly the same colour. Cuckoos lay eggs that look like the eggs of their host, so the host does not notice the new egg.

The Cuckoo's egg hatches before the others. When the chick is a few days old, and still naked and blind, it heaves the Reed Warbler's eggs out of the nest.

The adult Reed Warblers bring insects to feed the young Cuckoo. They put the food into its huge gaping beak. They believe the Cuckoo is their own chick.

Reed Warbler

Cuckoo chick

The Cuckoo grows very fast and it is soon bursting out of the nest. It is now much bigger than its foster parents, who have to stand on its back to feed it.

Roadrunners

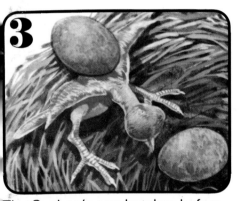

This bird lives in hot dry places in North and Central America. It runs fast and uses its tail as a rudder to swerve quickly and change direction. It eats insects, lizards and snakes.

Turacos

Schalow's Turaco

Turacos live in dense forests in Africa. They run along branches, hopping from tree to tree, and fly the short distances which are too far to jump. They live on fruits, berries and insects.

Parrots

Parrots are very noisy, brightly coloured birds. There are over 300 species and most live in tropical jungles. They have hooked beaks which they can use when climbing. Most Parrots live in trees and many have loud, shrieking voices.

Scarlet Macaw
(1 m long)

Nesting

Western Rosella

Most Parrots nest in holes in trees or termite mounds where the chicks are well hidden from enemies. They often use holes left by Woodpeckers or other birds.

Monk Parakeet

Groups of Monk (or Quaker) Parakeets collect thorny twigs and branches to build a huge shared nest. Each pair has its own nest chamber and entrance hall.

Macaws are the largest Parrots. They have very long tails which stream out behind them when they fly. Macaws live in South America and eat nuts, berries and fruits.

Pygmy Parrots

Finsch's Pygmy Parrot (10 cm long)

The six species of Pygmy Parrots are tiny. Their long claws and stiff tails help them climb up and down trees like Woodpeckers.

Budgerigars

Wedge-tailed Eagle

Budgerigars at a water hole

Budgerigars live in Australia and collect in enormous flocks. Each Budgerigar stays with the group because, as part of a great mass of flying birds, it is less likely to be caught by a bird of prey.

Budgerigars feed on grass seeds and drink at water holes together. Sometimes thousands of them die because a drought dries up the water holes and prevents their food from growing.

Budgerigars were first brought to Europe in 1840 and they became popular pets. Blue and yellow Budgerigars have been specially bred—in the wild they are always green.

1 Feeding

Black Cockatoo

Most Parrots have a thick, fleshy tongue. They hold a seed or nut in the top part of the beak with their tongue, and crack it with the lower part of the beak.

2

Rainbow Lorikeet

Lorikeets feed on nectar in flowers. The brush-like hairs on their tongues pick up pollen too. The Lorikeet brushes this pollen on to another flower and so helps pollinate it.

3

Greater Sulphur-crested Cockatoo

Cockatoos, like other Parrots, can use their claws like a hand to pick up food. Cockatoos live in flocks, and feed and roost together.

Talking

African Grey Parrot

The African Grey probably imitates human speech better than any other Parrot, but it does not understand the meaning of the words it copies.

Keas

The Kea of New Zealand is more like a bird of prey than a Parrot. As well as eating leaves and berries, it eats dead flesh which it tears with its long, curved bill. It gets its name from its call—"Kea-ea-ea".

Kakapos

The Kakapo or Owl-Parrot is nocturnal and has a flat owlish face. By day it sleeps in hollows under trees. It cannot fly and so is in danger from stoats and rats. It is one of the world's rarest birds.

35

Owls

Owls never gather in flocks. They are meat-eaters and catch all sorts of animals—small mammals, insects, frogs, snakes and fish. There are about 130 species of Owls and different ones are found in most parts of the world. Some Eagle Owls are almost a metre high and some Least Pygmy Owls are only 12 cm high.

Owls seize their prey with their sharp claws and kill with their strong hooked beaks.

Barn Owl with Field Mouse

Tengmalm's Owl

Some Owls nest in tree holes made by Woodpeckers. During the day they roost in these holes.

Most Owls hunt by night. Some can catch their prey in total darkness, by sound alone. They hoot to warn other Owls away from their territory and to call to each other. When food is scarce, they may hunt in the daytime.

How Owls Hunt at Night

1 Feathers

Scops Owl

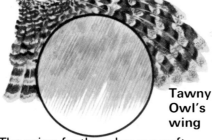

Tawny Owl's wing

Many Owls have drab brown plumage which camouflages them from their prey. Their dull feathers do not catch the light.

The wing feathers have a soft, fringed edge, which helps make Owls' flight silent. This picture shows the edge of a Tawny Owl's wing in close-up.

2 Eyes

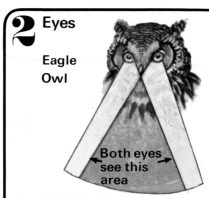

Eagle Owl

Both eyes see this area

Owls' vision is sharper than that of most birds. Their eyes are at the front of the head, not at the side. Owls use both eyes to look at the same area.

Snowy Owls

Arctic Skua

Snowy Owls live in the far north where they hunt small mammals called lemmings, and Arctic hares. The female's plumage camouflages her on patchy snow. She lays her eggs in a scrape in the ground. The male brings her food while she sits on the eggs. Although the parents try to protect the chicks, many may be killed by Arctic foxes and Skuas.

Pellets

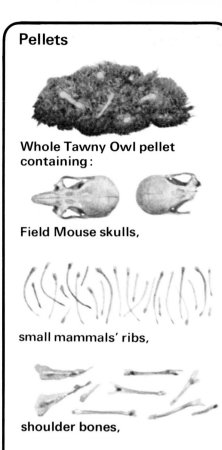

Whole Tawny Owl pellet containing:

Field Mouse skulls,

small mammals' ribs,

shoulder bones,

legs, feet and back-bones.

Owls swallow their prey whole. Later they cough up the parts they cannot digest in a pellet. The pictures above show the contents of a Tawny Owl's pellet.

Short-eared Owl

Owls cannot move their eyes in their sockets at all, but they can turn their heads in almost any direction—even upside down!

3 Ears

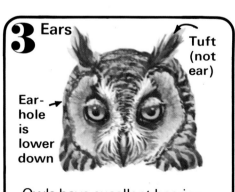

Tuft (not ear)

Ear-hole is lower down

Owls have excellent hearing. Their ear holes are very big and can pick up tiny sounds, like the squeaking of a mouse. The tufts on their heads are nothing to do with ears.

Elf Owls

The adult Elf Owl is smaller than a Sparrow. It often nests in an empty Woodpecker hole made in the huge Saguaro cactus. When the Elf owlets hatch they are only about 25 mm long.

Swifts, Swallows and Martins

Swifts, Swallows and Martins all behave in the same way, although Swifts belong to a different Family.

They all have long, swept-back wings and streamlined bodies and spend most of their time in the air where they catch flying insects in their gaping beaks. Many species migrate thousands of miles north from Africa and South America to breed in Europe and North America.

To save making lots of trips when they are feeding their young, Swifts collect hundreds of insects in their throats. They take this food ball back to the nest.

Swifts have been known to fly up to 95 kph. They can easily escape from Hawks and other birds of prey.

Their eyes are set deep in their heads. This stops flying dust getting into them.

Common Swift

They tuck their short legs into their feathers, like aeroplane wheels. Their legs are weak and they can hardly walk.

When Swifts touch down, they cling to an upright surface like a wall or a tree. They climb with their toes pointing forwards and take off by dropping down into the air.

Swifts are believed to sleep on the wing. They only come down to nest.

Nests

The Common Palm Swift sticks feathers and plant material together with spit to make its nest on a palm leaf. It cements the eggs into the nest in the same way.

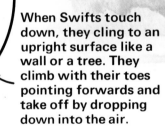

Sand Martins scrabble with their toes in sandy banks to scoop out their nest tunnels. The tunnel is about a metre long and has a little nest chamber at the end.

Swallows make their nests in buildings. They base the nest on a beam or a nail. They make pellets out of mud and build these up into a cup-shaped nest.

Hummingbirds

There are over 300 species of Hummingbirds and most are about 9 cm long from beak to tail. The Cuban Bee Hummingbird is the smallest known bird and measures only 5.7 cm.

Hummingbirds are only found in the Americas and most of them live in the tropical forests of South America. Their beautiful plumage reflects the light and changes colour as they dart about.

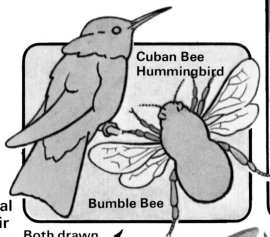

Cuban Bee Hummingbird

Bumble Bee

Both drawn life size

Flying

Hummingbirds can hover when they feed. They beat their wings back and forth in a figure of eight movement to do this, not up and down like other birds.

The special shapes of their long thin beaks are good for probing into different flowers for nectar.

Sword-billed Hummingbird

Buff-tailed Sicklebill

Broad-billed Hummingbird

1 Nests

Many female Hummingbirds spend a long time building their tiny nests. They make them with cobwebs, moss, leaves, petals and feathers.

2

When the two white eggs are laid, the female camouflages the nest with moss and lichen. She feeds the chicks on nectar. In most species, the male takes no part in rearing the young.

Hummingbirds get their name because they beat their wings so fast (over 100 beats per second) that they make a humming sound like a bee. They use up such an enormous amount of energy flying that they need to eat a great deal. They suck nectar from thousands of flowers and eat hundreds of insects every day.

Kingfishers

Kingfishers are small hole-nesting birds. There are more than 80 species and they are found all over the world, except in the far north and far south. Many live near water where they dive for fish, catching them with their spear-like beaks. Other species of Kingfishers, like Kookaburras, eat insects and reptiles.

Most Kingfishers are very brightly coloured, though if you see one flying, it moves so fast it is just a blur of colour.

Kookaburras

Kookaburras are well known in the Australian bush for their wild "laughing" chorus which is heard at dawn and dusk. One bird begins and others join in until they are all "laughing" loudly.

Bee-eaters

Rainbow Bee-eater

Bee-eaters are colourful birds related to Kingfishers. Most species live in tropical places in Asia, Africa and Australia. They gather in large flocks and feed on bees and other insects.

1 Kingfishers

The male Kingfisher waits on a branch until he sees a fish in the water. In a flash, he dives down and seizes it in his beak. He may bash it on a branch to stop it flapping and kill it.

2

Female   Male

In early spring the male courts the female by giving her a fish. He offers it to her head first so that she can swallow it easily. Together they dig out a nest tunnel in the river bank.

3   Male

Female

The male hovers above the female and lands on her back to mate. He holds on to her neck with his beak and flaps his wings to keep his balance. After mating, the eggs start to grow inside the female.

4

The female lays about six white eggs in the nest chamber at the end of the tunnel. The eggs hatch in three weeks. The chicks are naked and blind. Their parents feed them with small fish.

5

The Kingfisher chicks grow fast. At first their feathers are covered in spiny quills. These soon split to let the feathers appear. Their first plumage is drabber than their parents', but after moulting in the autumn they grow bright new feathers. The young leave the nest about a month after they hatch.

Hornbills

Most Hornbills have a large bill and many have a casque on their bill. Although the casque can be bigger than the bill itself, casques are usually hollow and therefore light. Most species of Hornbills live in forests in Africa and Asia, although some are found in open country. Hornbills eat fruit, such as passion fruit, figs and berries, insects and lizards.

Great Indian Hornbill

Casque

It is possible that the casque helps the Hornbill to attract a mate. It does not seem to have any other use.

1 Red-billed Hornbills

Red-billed Hornbills make their nest in a hollow tree. They collect pellets of mud to wall up the tree hole. Then the female gets inside and seals up the hole with mud that has fallen into it, leaving only a narrow slit.

2 Male / Female

The female lays two to five eggs inside the tree. The male brings her insects, fruit and lizards, and feeds them to her through the slit. While she is inside the tree hole, she moults and pushes the feathers out through the hole.

3 Female

The Hornbill feeds her naked chicks with food which the male passes in to her. She keeps the nest clean by using the chicks' droppings to strengthen the mud wall. The chicks are safe from birds of prey and monkeys.

4 Female

When the chicks are old enough and her new feathers have grown, the female pecks away the mud wall. Then she flies out of the nest. She helps the male collect food to take to the young, who stay in the nest-hole.

5 Chicks

When their mother has left, the chicks seal up the hole again, still leaving a small gap through which food can be passed by the parents. The young birds' bills are pale orange, but will turn red by the time they are mature.

6 Adult / Chick

Six weeks after hatching, the chicks have grown their flight feathers. One of them breaks open the mud wall and makes its first clumsy flight. The others follow, while the parents sit on the tree squawking encouragement.

Woodpeckers

There are over 200 species of Woodpeckers in the world. Most of them make nesting holes in trees each year, but this is not the only cause of the loud tapping sounds that you can hear in woods. As well as using their bills for chipping away at tree trunks, Woodpeckers drum on hollow branches to attract a mate, and to warn off other birds.

Woodpeckers do not hurt themselves when they hammer at trees, because their heads and necks are specially adapted to take the shock.

Most Woodpeckers have two toes pointing forward and two pointing back on each foot. This arrangement is good for climbing and clinging on to tree trunks.

Greater Spotted Woodpeckers

Most Woodpeckers use their strong tails to help keep them upright when they are clinging to a tree.

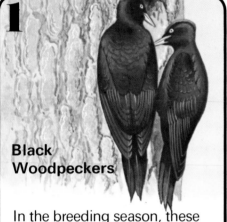

1

Black Woodpeckers

In the breeding season, these Woodpeckers make nesting holes in trees. The male and female take turns to bore into the trunk, or to enlarge a hole already there.

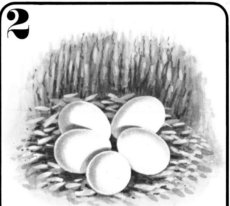

2

Some of the chippings from the hollowed-out tree form the lining of the nest. The eggs hatch in about twelve days and the chicks are blind at first.

3

The parents hang upside-down in the hole to feed the chicks. They stick their bills right down the chicks' throats.

4

When the chicks are older, they come to the hole to be fed. They leave the nest after about a month and do not return.

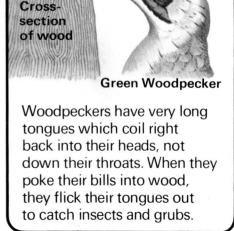

Cross-section of wood

Green Woodpecker

Woodpeckers have very long tongues which coil right back into their heads, not down their throats. When they poke their bills into wood, they flick their tongues out to catch insects and grubs.

Toucans and Barbets

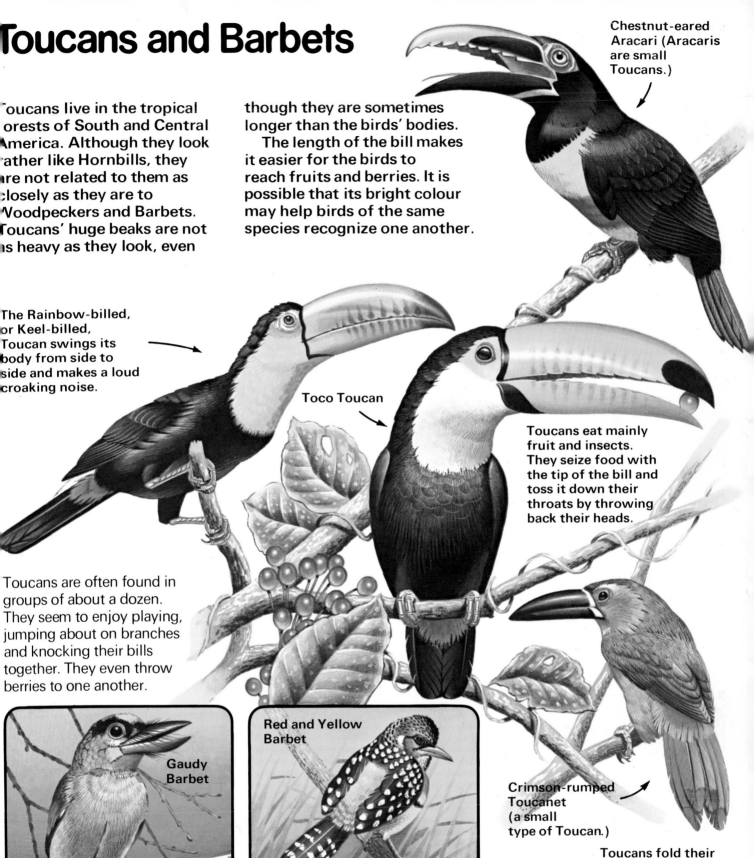

Toucans live in the tropical forests of South and Central America. Although they look rather like Hornbills, they are not related to them as closely as they are to Woodpeckers and Barbets. Toucans' huge beaks are not as heavy as they look, even though they are sometimes longer than the birds' bodies.

The length of the bill makes it easier for the birds to reach fruits and berries. It is possible that its bright colour may help birds of the same species recognize one another.

Chestnut-eared Aracari (Aracaris are small Toucans.)

The Rainbow-billed, or Keel-billed, Toucan swings its body from side to side and makes a loud croaking noise.

Toco Toucan

Toucans eat mainly fruit and insects. They seize food with the tip of the bill and toss it down their throats by throwing back their heads.

Toucans are often found in groups of about a dozen. They seem to enjoy playing, jumping about on branches and knocking their bills together. They even throw berries to one another.

Gaudy Barbet

Red and Yellow Barbet

Crimson-rumped Toucanet (a small type of Toucan.)

Toucans fold their tails up over their backs when resting. Like this they can sit comfortably in tree holes, where they nest.

Barbets live in South America, Africa and Asia. They are small, brightly coloured birds and live mainly on fruits and insects. They make holes for nesting and sometimes for roosting.

D'Arnaud's Barbets burrow in sandy soil, and Red and Yellow Barbets dig holes in termite mounds or in sandy banks. Other kinds of Barbets hollow out rotten tree trunks.

43

Perching Birds

There are over 5,000 kinds of perching birds, including such different species as the Birds of Paradise and birds like Swallows and Martins (see page 38), Thrushes and Blackbirds.

All perching birds' feet are well adapted for perching, with three toes pointing forwards and one backwards. They all have a similar bone structure and most of them are naked and helpless when they hatch. Scientists have grouped them together into an order (see page 6) called Passeriformes.

Birds of Paradise

The male birds perform a fantastic courtship dance.

Birds of Paradise are so beautiful that when they were first brought to Europe people believed they came from paradise. In fact, most of these birds live deep in the forests of New Guinea and neighbouring islands. The male is very colourful, but the female's plumage is a drab brown.

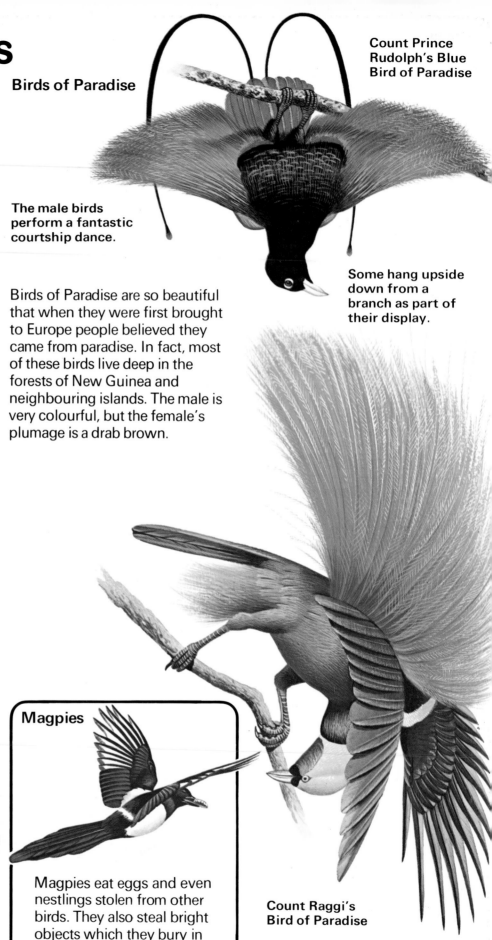

Count Prince Rudolph's Blue Bird of Paradise

Some hang upside down from a branch as part of their display.

Count Raggi's Bird of Paradise

House Sparrows

Female

Male

House Sparrows are typical Passeriformes and are often seen in towns and cities where they feed on scraps.

Jays

This Jay has a beakful of ants and is rubbing them on its feathers. Other birds also do this. Formic acid on the ants is believed to kill the mites on the Jay's body.

Magpies

Magpies eat eggs and even nestlings stolen from other birds. They also steal bright objects which they bury in the ground or take back to their nests.

Bowerbirds

Bowerbirds live in New Guinea and Australia. Most male Bowerbirds build a bower, or stage, on the ground to attract a female. They decorate it with colourful objects like flowers, shells, pebbles, shiny beetle cases and even bottle tops. The bower is not a nest. The male calls to the female and dances in front of the bower with a bright object in his beak. After mating, the female builds the nest in a tree.

The male Satin Bowerbird builds an avenue with twigs woven together. With a mixture of spit and charcoal, he paints

Satin Bowerbirds

Male

Female

the wall of the bower, using a piece of bark as a paintbrush.

He collects blue objects to decorate the bower's entrance.

Blue Tits

Blue Tits tear holes in milk bottle tops and drink the cream. This is a good example of a bird learning a skill which helps it survive.

Cocks of the Rock

This male bird has a crest on its head which almost covers its beak. To attract females, the males choose a clearing in the forest in which to show off their plumage.

Strange Nests

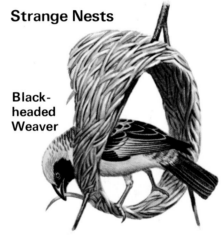

Black-headed Weaver

The male Weaver makes a nest out of grasses and strips of leaf. He builds outwards from a ring of grass until the nest is like a ball with a sock-shaped entrance-tunnel hanging down from it.

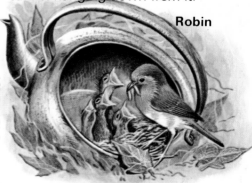

Robin

Dippers

The Dipper stands on rocks in streams, dipping its head and bobbing up and down. When it sees its prey, the Dipper

dives into the water. It can walk along the river bed, catching insects and fish in its beak.

In woodlands, Robins nest in hidden holes, but garden Robins often find that an old bucket or kettle makes a good nesting place.

Bird Facts and Figures

Species	Average size (Length = beak to tail tip)	Where the bird lives	Main foods	Nest	Average number of eggs laid
Ostrich	2 m high	Open bush country	Vegetation, small mammals	Scrape on ground	6–8
Emperor Penguin	1.3 m high	Antarctic sea ice	Fish	Makes no nest. Lays egg on ice	1
Great Crested Grebe	48 cm long	Lakes	Fish	Floating reed nest	3–6
Great Northern Diver	75 cm long	Northern seas	Fish	Reed nest on bank of lake	2
White Pelican	1.5 m long	Shallow rivers and lakes	Fish	Nest of debris on ground	1–2
Guanay Cormorant	75 cm long	Coasts of Chile and Peru	Fish	Nest of debris scraped in guano	3
White Stork	1 m long	Open grasslands and marshes	Frogs, reptiles, small mammals, insects	Stick nest, often on building	3–5
Grey Heron	90 cm long	Rivers and ponds	Fish, frogs	Stick nest in tree	3–5
Greater Flamingo	1.5 m long	Flat coastal waters and inland lakes	Tiny water animals	Mud nest in shallow water	1–2
Mute Swan	1.5 m long	Rivers, lakes and ponds	Water plants	Large nest on ground by water	5–7
Greylag Goose	80 cm long	Lakes, marshes and grasslands	Seeds and small water creatures	Plant nest on marshy ground	4–8
Mallard Duck	58 cm long	Inland water, ponds in parks	Water and land plants	Nest on ground or sometimes in tree	7–14
Golden Eagle	85 cm long	Mountains and moorlands	Mammals and birds	Stick nest on cliff or in tall tree	2
African White-backed Vulture	80 cm long	Open plains	Dead flesh of zebra, antelope, etc.	Stick nest in tree	1
Common Pheasant	male 80 cm female 60 cm	Farmland	Plants, seeds and berries	Hidden scrape on ground	6–19
Red Jungle Fowl	male 70 cm female 30 cm	Forests	Grain, bamboo, seeds, insects	Hidden scrape on ground	5–6
Oystercatcher	43 cm long	Mudflats, seashore	Mussels and other shellfish	Scrape on beach, lined with shells or pebbles	3
Sarus Crane	1.5 m long	Grassy plains and marshes	Grain, berries, insects, fish	Plant nest on marshy ground	2
Herring Gull	60 cm long	Sea cliffs and dunes, farmland	Fish, shellfish, scraps	Shallow nest on cliff or sand	2–3
Little Tern	24 cm long	Sandy beaches and dunes	Small fish	Scrape on beach, edged with pebbles	2–3
Puffin	30 cm long	Rocky islands and coasts	Small fish	Burrow on cliff top	1
Woodpigeon	41 cm long	Woods and farmland	Grain, seeds, berries and buds	Twig nest in tree	2
Common Cuckoo	33 cm long	Woods, farmland, heaths	Caterpillars and other insects	Lays eggs in other birds' nests	6–18
African Grey Parrot	35 cm long	Forests	Seeds and fruit	Tree hole	2–4
Barn Owl	34 cm long	Woods and farmland	Small mammals, small birds and insects	In tree or building	4–7
Common Swift	16 cm long	In the air	Flying insects	Under eaves of building	2–3
Ruby-throated Hummingbird	9 cm long	Woods, gardens	Small insects and nectar	Cup nest in tree	2
Kingfisher	16 cm long	Rivers and streams	Fish	Tunnel in river bank	6–7
Great Indian Hornbill	1.3 m long	Forests	Fruit	Large hollow in tree	2
Green Woodpecker	32 cm long	Woodlands	Insects and insect larvae	Hole drilled in tree	5–8
Keel-billed Toucan	38 cm long	Tropical forests	Fruit	Tree hole	3
House Sparrow	14 cm long	Towns, farmland	Scraps, seeds, grain, insects	Grass and debris nest in trees and buildings	3–6
Count Raggi's Bird of Paradise	35 cm long	Forests	Fruit	Nest in fork between branches of tree	1–2

Index

PRINTED IN BELGIUM BY

proost

INTERNATIONAL BOOK PRODUCTION